I0494684

Quick Tips from a Pro Photographer

Book 9

Flowers

By Julia K Harwood

Table of Contents

Introduction

Flowers come in all shapes and sizes from tiny trigger plants to the larger frangipani or hippeastrum's, so we need to go from macro photography through to ordinary photography.

If you want to take the smaller flowers close up or parts of a flower, then I recommend my Quick Tips from a Pro Photographer Book 8 - Macro.

http://www.amazon.com.au/Macro-Photography-Quick-Tips-Photographer-ebook/dp/B015J5S74G
This covers all the intricate details we need to know for Macro.

Here I will cover general flower photography and images you can take with your normal lenses.

You can also use a point and shoot camera or even the modern smart phones take great photos.

So you should never be without a camera to grab that special flower when you see it.

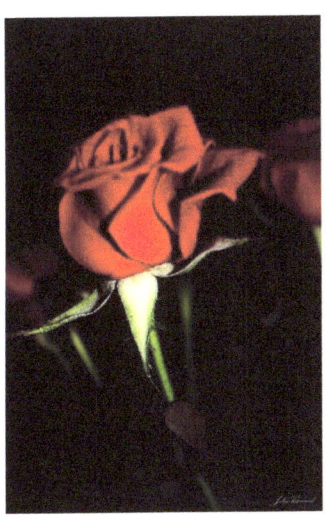

Secret to perfect photos of flowers.

What is the secret?

It's actually very simple and achievable by everyone.
Here it is:
Start with the perfect flower.

This sounds basic, but often looking for that flawless flower or one that only has little blemishes that you can erase in post processing is what will be the difference between a nice photo and a great flower image.

This is often the overlooked part that leaves you struggling to get that perfect image

Weather

Weather is very important if we are photographing flowers in a garden or outdoors. We need to look at the wind, rain, cloud, sunshine, frost and more.

If we take the flower indoors to take the photo, then you have total control over this element.

However, flowers often look best with some of the natural habitat around and you can use natural light as opposed to indoors having to create the right light.

Sometimes as with wildflowers you are not allowed to pick them, so indoors photography is not an option.

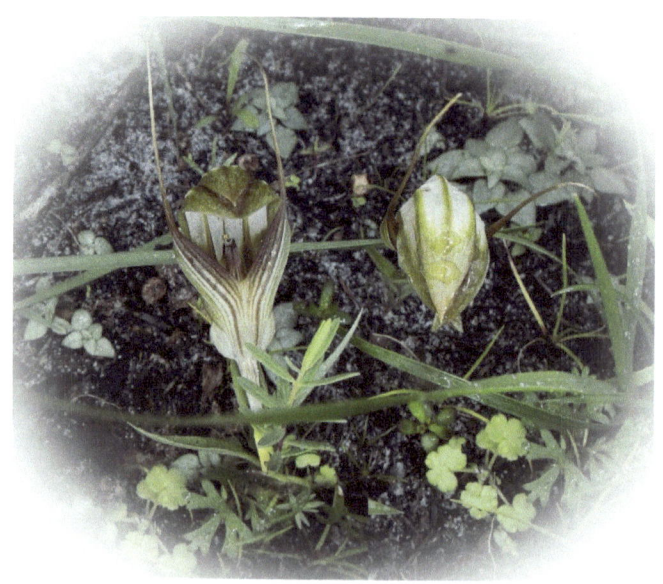

There is a great app called "Clear Outside" that gives us a way of planning and preparing for whatever the weather will be.

Wind

Flower photography's worst enemy is the wind.

On windy days you need a high shutter speed to get the motion to freeze.

To do this often means shooting in the middle of the day when the sun is at its brightest, but that then washes out the colors.

Alternatively, you can increase your ISO but this can introduce noise in the image and also softens the image a little, so how do we get around this?

We pick the time of the day when the wind is its lowest.
Using an app will help with this.

Also, usually first thing in the morning there is less wind.

You get a double bonus here as at this time of the day, the light is also nice and soft and coming from the side so that it enhances the detail.

The other bonus is you may get some morning dew to add that extra something to your shot.

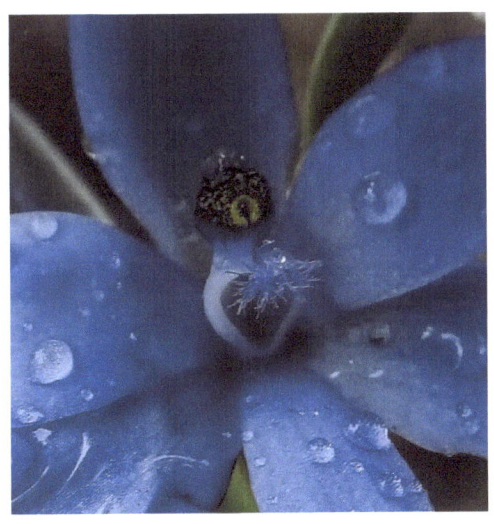

Another way around wind is to make a wind break. Some black foam board bent so that it has two sides and a back can stop the wind and provide you with an uncluttered background.

Cloud

Cloudy days will become your best friend, as cloud turns the sky into a giant soft box and the light is nice and even and the colors become fully saturated.

I use these days for my close up shots. If I am going to shoot a garden or fields of flowers I will try to have some blue sky to add a nice contrast and some interest in that part of the image.

But for macro, close-up shots or shots that don't include the sky, the lovely even lighting of a cloudy day is perfect.

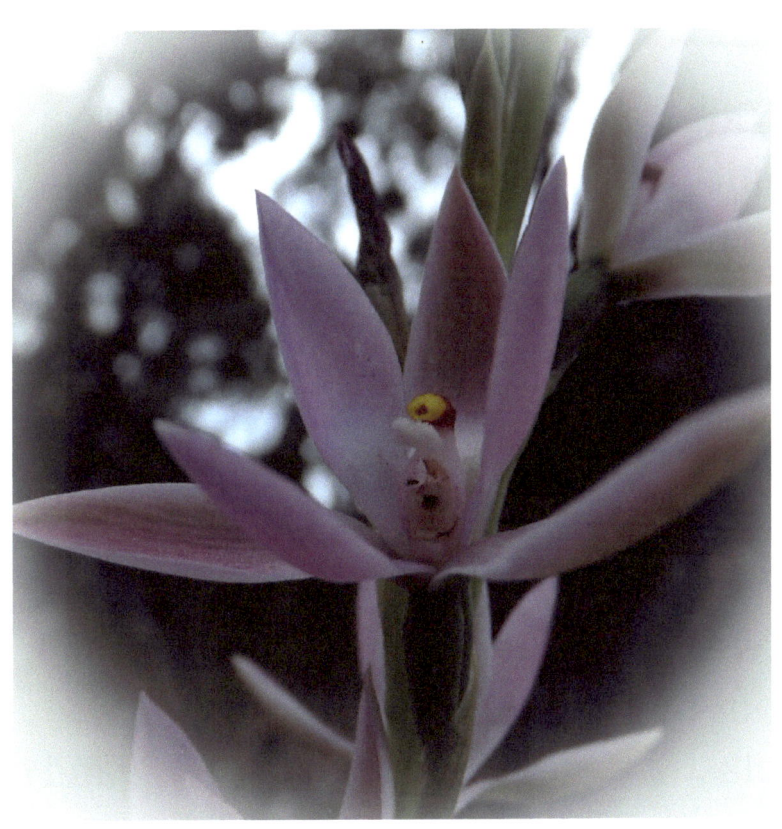

Rain

Rain can create some unique and intriguing images of flowers. You can shoot from under cover or through a window or out under an umbrella.

A note of caution here, remember to ensure your camera stays dry. If you have a shower cap you can put this over the camera and let the lens stick out of the opening, then put an elastic band around the opening and the lens to hold it is place and protect the lens. This also works with freezer bags.

Rain drops reflect and magnify. You can use this to create great images.

So make sure the drops are not too bright and also see if you can position yourself so that you can see something in the drops.

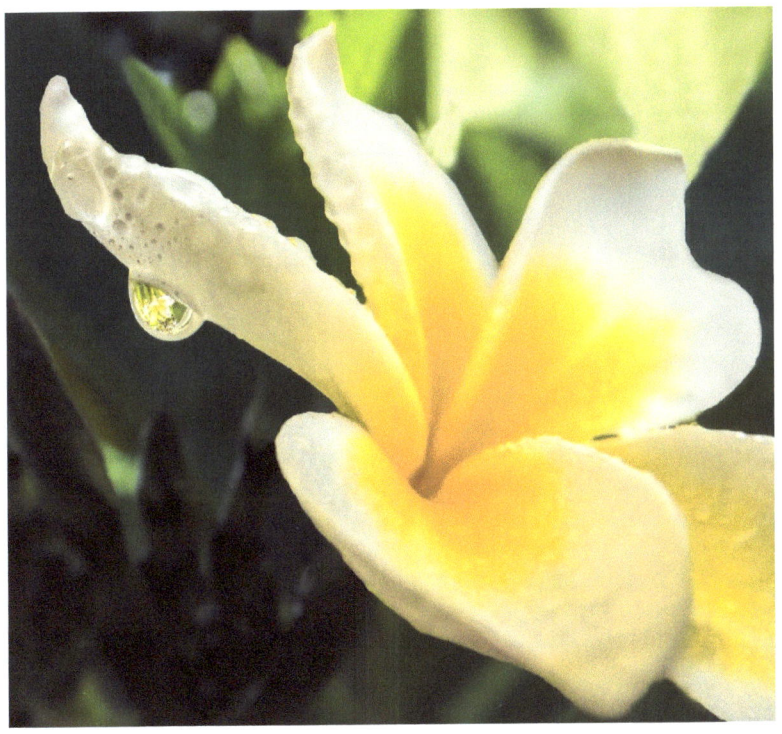

Sunshine

The sun gives us beautiful natural light, but we need to be aware of its properties.

In the morning and evening the sunlight has a warm or golden hue to it, during the rest of the day it has a cool or blue hue.

It is important to set your white balance to match the light to get a proper reproduction of the color.

You can choose your setting from sunshine, cloudy, beach, snow, etc., so choose the one that most matches the light at the site you are photographing the flowers.

Light, when on an angle, again morning and afternoon, shows up more detail so we get the veins in the leaves and the details in the flowers.

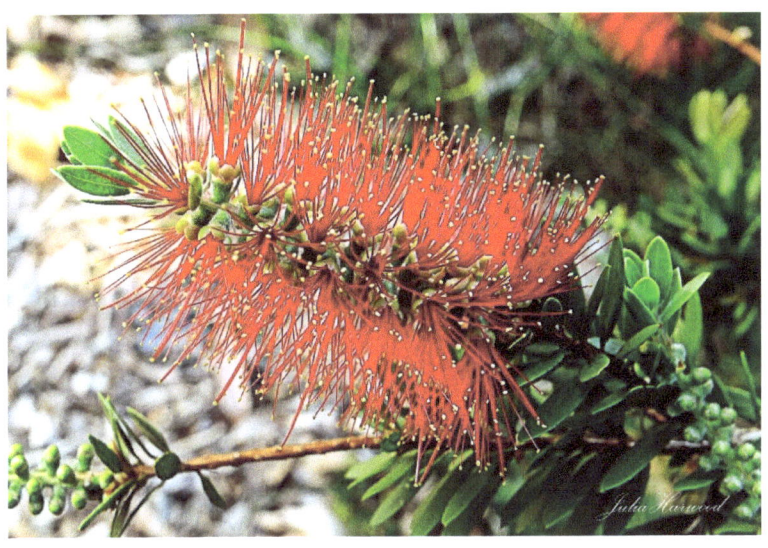

It also intensifies the color.
You need to watch for and be aware of shadows at these times.

The midday sun is very bright and harsh so it tends to wash colors out. Sometimes it works to use this though as there are no shadows and you can use a faster shutter speed.

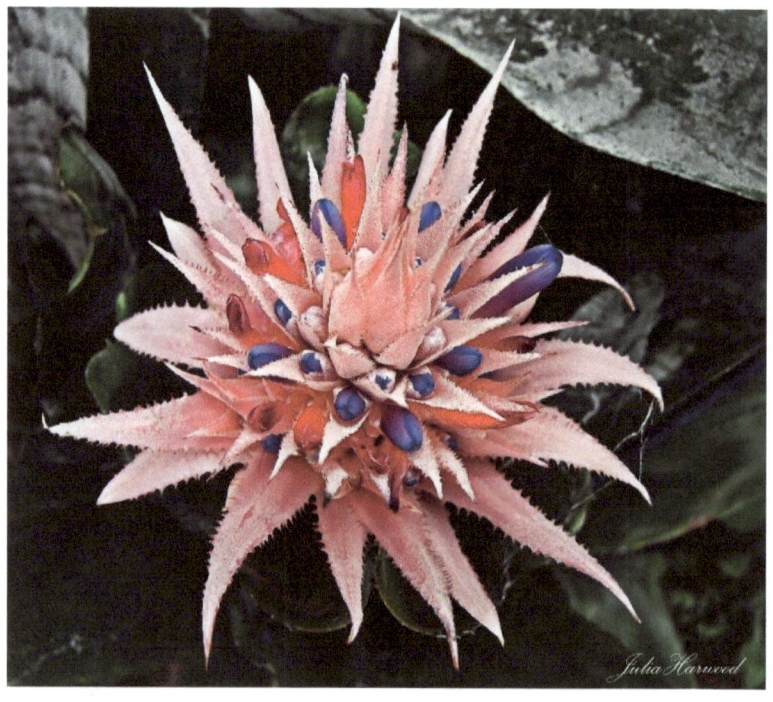

Just remember to add some more vibrance in post processing

Frost and snow

Again these can create some unusual images, but we need to be aware that the snow is very bright and will trick the cameras auto white balance so you need to set it manually.

The same applies here as for wet weather, protect your camera. Also the batteries will run down quickly in cold weather so put spare batteries close to your skin to keep them warm.

Frost can create great patterns and really can add a fantastic element to include in the shot if you have frost in your area.

Composition.

For an in depth look at composition be sure to get my book on Composition.

http://www.amazon.com.au/Composition-Quick-Tips-Photographer-Book-ebook/dp/B00WXH49AU

But here we will look at some basics of composition we use in flower Photography.

We need to think about what aspect ratio to use, do we use rule of thirds, triangle or even spiral instead.

Then we need to look at color, shape and form.

Angles to shoot from and what to include and exclude.

What can I use to add even more?

Let's start with overall composition and *aspect ratios*.

If we are shooting a single bloom you will often find filling the frame works best and we see a lot of images like this, where one flower fills the entire frame.

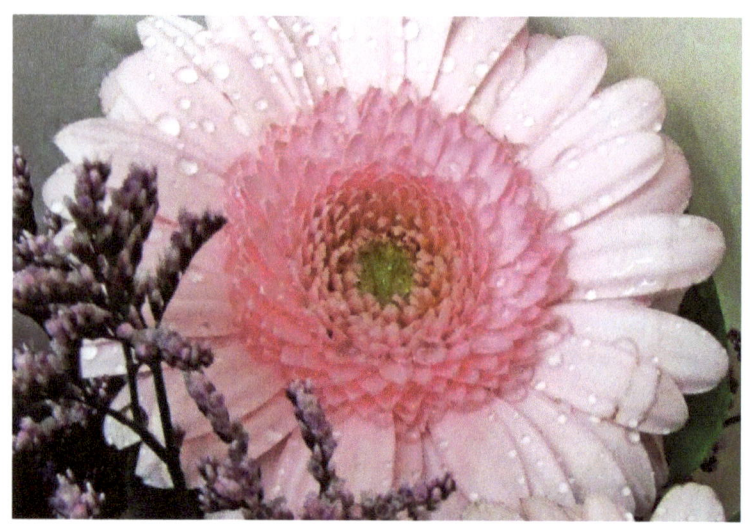

But if you are shooting a bunch of flowers on a plant can you see a branch that will act as a leading line taking us to the flowers?

Do the flowers look best off to one side a bit?

If you are taking more than one flower, look for symmetry or otherwise try for the rule of odds.

This is where you have an odd number of flowers or an odd number of petals, as it draws the person's eye to the flowers between the others as well as adds a certain tension to the image which will hold the viewer for longer.

One of the aspect ratios that is used more in flower photography that any other subject is the spiral rule. Here are some examples of the spiral aspect ratio in flowers.

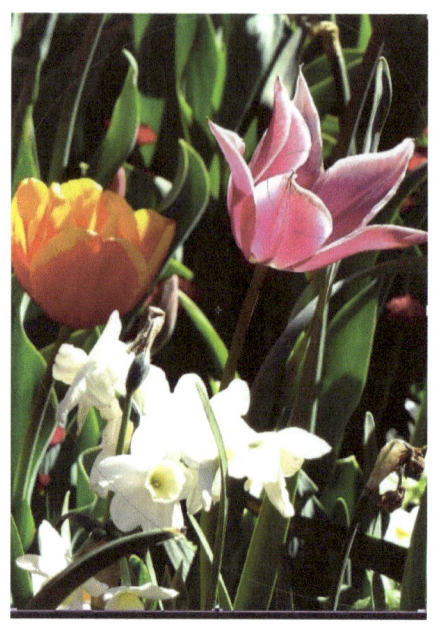

The image above shows the rule of odds and the spiral aspect ratio.

Also experiment with a square crop.

Then let's look at *color*.
Look for complimentary colors for the background.

Complimentary colors are the ones opposite each other on the color wheel.

Red and green, purple and yellow, blue and orange are all complimentary colors.

So, if it is a red flower try to angle the shot so that the green foliage is in the background.

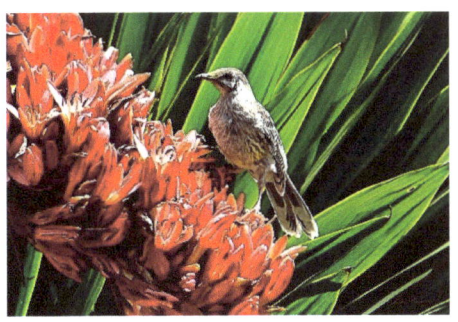

If an orange flower, use a lower angle to isolate it against the sky, or for a yellow look for some purple to put in the background.

We will often find complimentary colors in the flowers themselves as well.

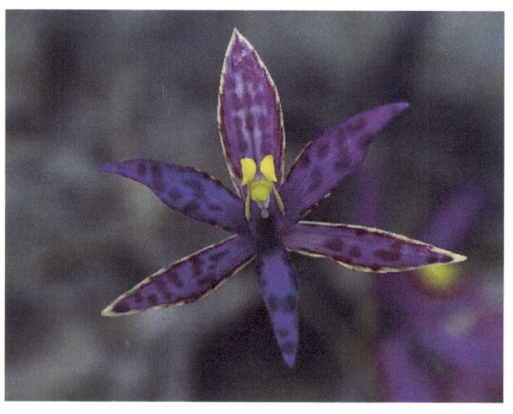

We can't always achieve this, but knowing your complimentary colors and looking for them will strengthen your image.

Isolate the flower

Another thing to try to do is isolate the flower.

If you are going for a single flower, try to isolate it so that it is not getting lost in amongst the other flowers.

We also do this by using a shallow depth of field, usually f4 or f5.6 works well.

You can try f2 or f2.8 but often you won't get the full flower in focus using the smallest depths of field.

Perspective and angle

Do you want just part of a flower or the full flower, just the buds or blossoms or full plant?
Stamen, pollen, faces in flowers...

Also look at different angles to shoot from, lay down and shoot up through the petals, this works really well if the sun is making them translucent.

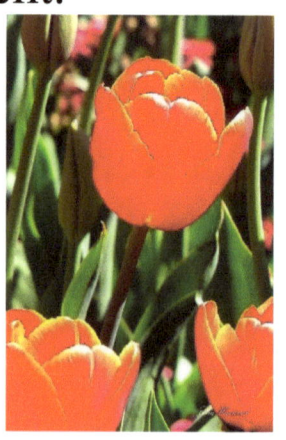

Look for bees and insects to add an additional composition element to the image or add water drops.

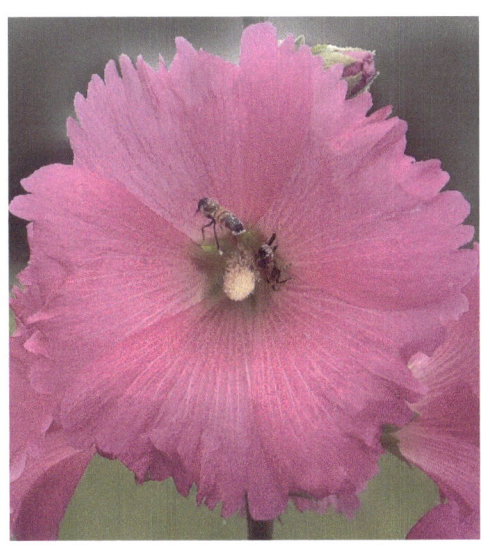

If you are lucky you may get natural dew drops or rain drops.

If not get a spray bottle and add glycerine to the water and spray the flower. The glycerine makes the drops hold to the flower.

Gear to use

Let's have a look at some of the gear you will need.

As I have said you can use a smart phone, a point and shoot camera, preferably one that captures RAW files as well as JPEG, a bridge camera or your DSLR.

There are two other bits of gear that I would highly recommend, the first is a tripod and the second is a ring flash.

A tripod will always give you sharper images, it also makes you take the time to look at the flower and really think about the composition.

It is not always practical to use a tripod, so use your common sense here and be careful not to damage the surrounding foliage, unless it is your own plant and you don't mind.

If you use your pop up flash or a flash on the hot shoe of your camera, then you will most likely get a shadow that is cast by your lens.

To avoid this, you can take the flash off the camera but then you still have light on one side and shadow on the other so to overcome this we use a ring flash.

A ring or macro flash allows you to add more light so that you can increase your shutter speed and freeze any motion.

This is important if you are in a heavily shaded area under trees or if there is a bit of wind.

It also comes in handy when trying to utilize that early morning or late afternoon light.

You may think you need a DSLR to get good flower photos, but current smart phones work well as do point and shoot cameras.

If you are serious about your photography, but want something light to carry with you then look for a point and shoot that shoots RAW as well as JPEG.

You can also get smart phones that shoot in RAW, the iPhone 6 does and also the Samsung Galaxy S6, HTC One and LG G4.

I would say most phones will soon have this feature so look at reviews to see which one is the best for photos. Also note that RAW uses a lot of memory, so make sure you can add additional memory via a memory card if you plan on using this option.

Another handy feature on a camera is a movable screen.

This allows you to put the camera down really low without you having to lie on the ground.

The big disadvantage of a point and shoot or a phone camera is not having a viewfinder, so on really bright days it is hard to see the LCD screen.

You can buy hoods to place over the screen to help with this.

You can also get little clip on lenses for the phones that give you macro, micro and telephoto which really makes them a very versatile camera alternative.

Also check out the many apps that are available.

On the iPhone if you touch the screen where you want the focus to be and hold it for a few seconds it will lock the focus and the exposure. When you touch the screen you will see a square with a light symbol next to it. You can drag the light symbol up and down to adjust the exposure.

Another issue with the point and shoot cameras is that sometimes it is hard to focus.

We don't have manual focus so the trick here is to find a piece of bark, a leaf or even a stick.

Hold this next to the flower and focus on this, half pressing the shutter or holding the spot on the phone to lock the focus here, then remove the stick, recompose and take the shot. You will have lovely sharp focus.

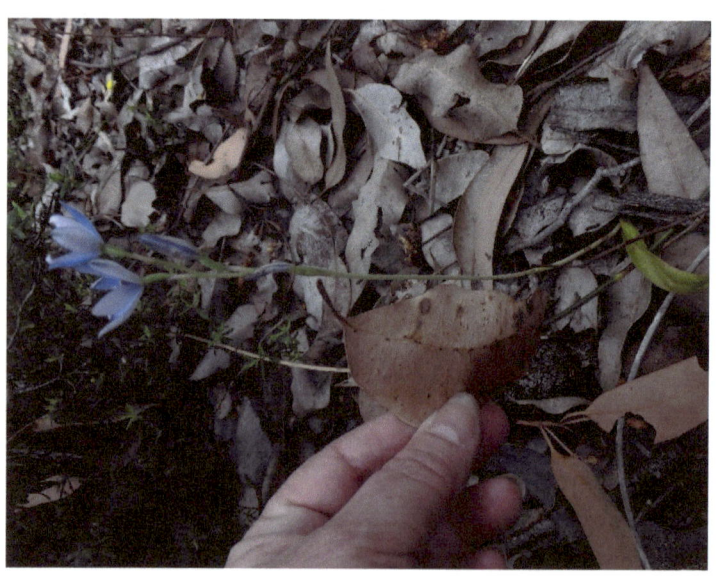

Remember practice makes perfect, so if at first you don't succeed, try and try again.

Finally, on the point and shoot and the DSLR you have scene modes and one of these is usually a flower, most of the time they will do a good job.

The advantage of the DSLR is that you can add a ring flash for low light situations.

When you use the auto scene mode check your image and see what settings it has used.

If less than 1/60 second, then put the camera on a tripod and reshoot. If it is windy you will need a shorter shutter speed to freeze the motion so you may need to go to shutter priority (S/Tv) or full manual (M) and choose a shutter speed of 1/120 or more.

I will cover settings more fully in the next chapter.

Settings

Depth of field

The first thing to think about when going to photograph a flower is how much do you want in focus.

Do you want the whole garden or just the one flower?

One consideration is how much is in the background, is it a busy garden or a bush area with all kinds of distractions, if this is the case then you would be best using a shallow depth of field, which means a large aperture or low f number.

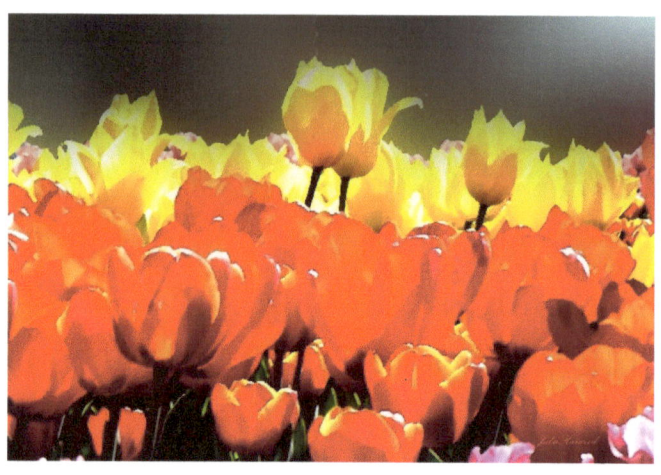

If it is an ordered garden that we want to show off, then use a large depth of field which is a small aperture or a high f number.

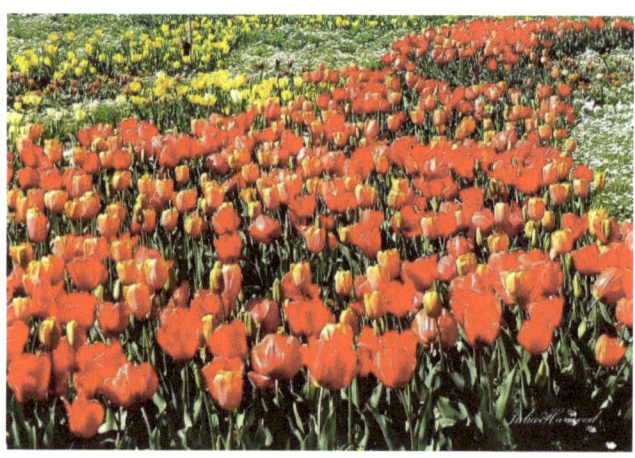

Shutter speed

The next thing we need to look at is shutter speed.

The main thing here is we want a fast enough shutter speed to freeze any motion, sometimes when it is really still we can get away 1/60 sec, but if there is a breeze then I would suggest 1/120.

This is one time when we can do something about it if it is one flower but not if it's the whole garden.

As previously mentioned you can make a wind break to help or if you have the option, move it to a sheltered area.

ISO

This is an important one.

Every camera handles ISO differently, so here is where you put this book down and grab your camera and do a test.

We may as well start with a flower, any one will do.

Start at ISO100 and take a shot, you can use the auto settings for this as long as it allows you to adjust the ISO.

Now take a series of images at all the different ISO settings. ISO100, 200, 400, 800,1600 etc.

Make sure you still keep the exposure correct.

Now head back indoors and load your images on the computer, open them up and view at 100%.

Go through them until you find where the cut off is for what you think is a sharp and clean enough image.

Then you will know you can safely go up to that ISO when trying to get a fast enough shutter speed.

Lighting

Natural lighting

A cloudy day is ideal for taking flower photos as it is like the whole sky is a soft box. This means the light is evenly dispersed and you won't get blown out highlights or dark shadows, it also means the colors will be more saturated.

The downside is there is less light so make sure you take your tripod with you.

You can also use natural lighting indoors if you have a window that lets enough light in, then turn off all the artificial lights and place the flowers near the window.

Time of day

This is important on days where there is no cloud cover.

It is also important for wind. There is usually less wind or breeze in the early morning and you will often also get dew on the flowers which intensifies the colors as well as adding another element to the image.

You can always add water to a flower at any time of the day just by having a spray bottle of water with you and mist the flower with it. If you want well-formed drops then use glycerine instead of water in your spray bottle or a mixture of water and glycerine.

Experiment and see what works best for you.

Remember, as mentioned before, water reflects, so watch out for reflections and make sure they add to the image rather than distract from it.

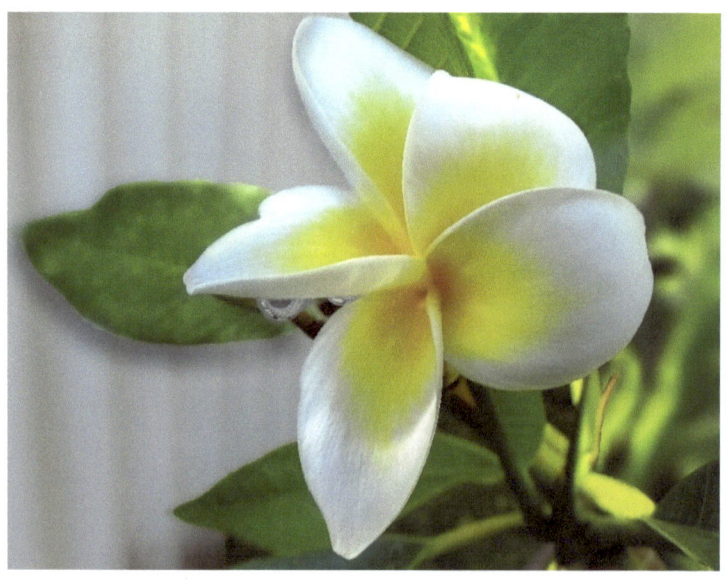

On a bright day avoid the middle of the day as the colors will be muted and you will have bright highlights and deep shadows, which does not make for very attractive images.

If you are out at this time, try to use your body to cast a shadow on the flower but only for close ups as we don't want to be aware of the shadow in the final image.

You can also use an umbrella as shade or a diffuser. A diffuser is the white semi-transparent piece that your reflectors zip onto.

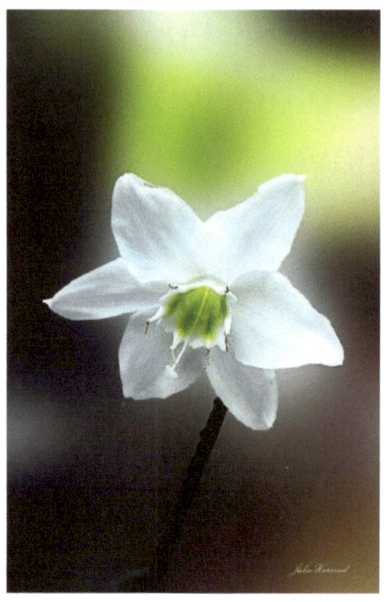

Holding this between the sun and the flower evens the light out.

This also helps if you are photographing a flower in a dappled light area.

While on the subject of reflectors, you can use these to add light by placing the reflector so that the light is bouncing off it and onto the flower, usually I place it slightly off to the side and at a 45-degree angle.

Move the reflector until you can see the light on the subject, then move it back a bit, this makes the light softer and nicer.

Remember if you want the details in the petals and leaves, then the best light is side light, so move your reflector to the side or shoot early in the morning or late in the afternoon.

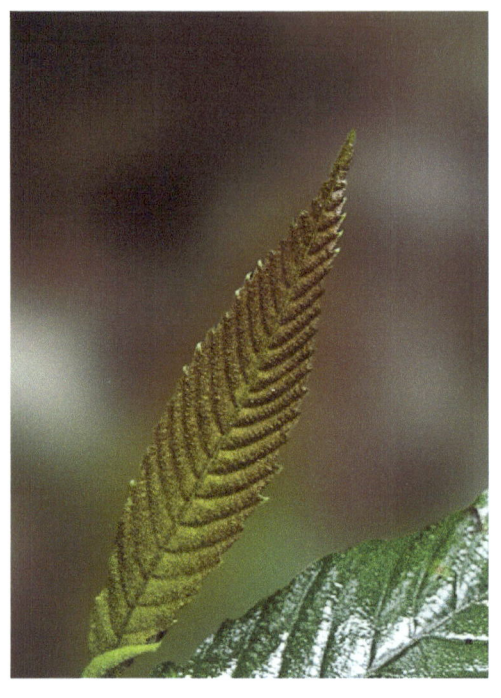

Red and yellow are very bright colors and often end up overexposed so if you are unsure of your exposure then bracket the image, there is usually a setting in the menu for you to do this, you want to bracket the exposure, so -2/3, 0, +2/3 or similar.

I always drop my exposure 1/2 to 1 stop whenever photographing red or yellow.

Remember most cameras have the ability to bring up the histogram display, so with this on the screen you can make sure that the histogram doesn't spike up on the right end, if it does then you need to decrease the exposure more.

Fill flash or ring flash

Flash can help us freeze the motion if there is a bit of wind, however, in flower photography it tends to wash the color out and create harsh shadows. So we use fill flash or ring flash to get around this.

Using fill flash adds that little bit of light without it being overpowering and a ring flash puts the light at the end of the lens so that you don't get any shadow from the lens, it also really helps to even out the light, meaning that you won't have over exposed highlights or dark shadows.

After a tripod my ring flash is the next most used piece of my kit for flower photography.

Indoor Lighting

You can always use natural lighting indoors but what if that is not available?

A light tent is often the best option, this allows you to isolate the flower and control the lighting and the background.

You can buy these quite cheap on-line or there are tutorials on how to make your own.

http://www.instructables.com/id/Photography-Light-Box/

https://www.youtube.com/watch?v=OyxzC5kqbyw

Conclusion

Finally remember to think outside the box, look for unusual angles, side on, front on, from above, from below, down at flower level.
The most important thing to look at here is the light. Photography is painting with light, so look for where the light is illuminating the flower or where it makes the flower look transparent.

When you see a flower you want to photograph, take a moment to see what it is about the flower that caught your attention, was it the color, the structure, the light?

Whatever it was that is what you want to make the focus of the image as it is what will hold the viewers' attention.

So try to take the image in such a way as to capture whatever it was that drew your attention in the first place.
Walk all around the flower, looking at it from all different angles, see how the light appears from different perspectives.

Sit with it for a moment, are there any bugs on it, do these add to the image, if so make sure they are in focus.

What if there are no gardens near you or it is too wet and windy?

Go and check out the local florist. You can buy a few flowers and photograph them inside or even better ask if you can take photos of their arrangements and offer them a copy that they can use for a website or brochure.

Florists usually have the lighting set up to show off the flowers so have a look at the way they are lit so that you can do a similar setup at home indoors.

Remember you can have fun and create abstracts too.

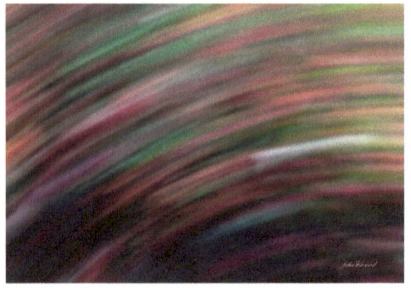

Special Thanks

I would like to make a special mention of a few people who without their support this series would not be possible.

Firstly, to my Proof Reader, Cathy Longley, no matter how sick you were you still managed to get these done, thank you so much.

Then to all my supporters on Pozible but most especially Angela Chan, as without her financial backing this project would not have been possible and finally to my wonderful husband Colin, who put up with me spending so many hours on the computer. I hope these help you on your photographic journey.

You can also follow me on my website at Photography by Julia K Harwood
http://www.juliaharwood.com/

For all your gift needs
http://www.redbubble.com/people/juliakharwood/portfolio

To follow me on G+
http://plus.google.com/+JuliaHarwood

To follow on FB
http://m.facebook.com/Photography.by.Julia.K.Harwood

To view a gallery of my images
http://photographybyjuliakharwood.shootproof.com/juliaharwood

Cheat Sheets

1. First look for a Perfect flower

2. Check the light

3. Check the background.
   -Go low to use sky as backdrop
   -Go high to use the ground
   -use black card to isolate flower

4. What will the weather be?

5. Is there wind?

6. What depth of field do I want?
   -low f number, narrow dof
   -high f number, large dof

7. Is shutter speed high enough

8. Use tripod if not.

9. Is this the best composition?
   -would spiral rule work?
   -can I use rule of odds?
   -Are there leading lines?
   -can you fill the frame?

10. What shadows are falling on the flower